What is a barbarian?

The term "barbarian" refers to one who has rejected or who is outside of "civilization".

Barbarians experience life to the fullest, unfettered by laws, social obligations, or embarrassment. They speak plainly, they enjoy life's pleasures voraciously, they love openly, and they fight savagely.

Most people think that because barbarians
are uncultured, impolite, or impulsive,
that they are unintelligent.

Let them think that.

Anger is your most powerful weapon.
Embrace it, and you will be deadlier than any dragon.

Anger is meant for enemies and monsters.
Being angry at a stone wall will only dull your
sword. Being angry at a friend will only cause
you to lose a friend. If you find yourself angry
at either a wall or a friend, calm yourself.
If you cannot calm yourself, leave the area.

Mere words should never make you angry.
You are under no obligation to argue with anyone.

It is possible to end an argument without conceding a point. Simply state that you disagree and do not wish to continue discussing the matter. No one can force you to speak.

Your anger should be like an explosion: powerful, decisive, and over quickly. If your anger is more like a smoldering fire that accomplishes nothing but lasts for hours, you do not have true anger - you have stress.

Stress is bad for you, get rid of it immediately.

It is important to take pleasure in simple things: a sunbeam, a hearty meal, a good joke. Life is short and joy is essential.

It is equally important to make sure those you love also take pleasure in whatever may give them joy. Be a good friend.

If a friend gives you a gift, accept it and enjoy it in every way you can. The gift of a friend, however small, is a piece of their love for you. Look for an opportunity to return that love to them in a new form.

If a stranger gives you a gift, do not accept it. The gift of a stranger, however small, contains many hooks. Though a stranger may offer you the whole world at no cost, in time you will find you have paid too much for it.

Do not break the sapling. The young, regardless of their starting point, have infinite potential to grow in new ways. Fighting a child is both evil and pointless.

Do not strike the mountain. The elderly either vastly outclass you or are harmless and will be dead soon. Fighting the elderly is both evil and pointless.

Running is good for the body, good for the mind, good for the soul, and you can do it for free. If possible, run every day.

If you are religious, you can pray while running. If you are creative, you can imagine while running. If you don't have an open flat area, climbing and swimming are also good.

Eat new things, and do not be fussy.
Experience every new taste you can. Your body is
not a temple, it's an animal - and it's omnivorous.

Although you should try as many different things as you can, there will be some experiences that aren't right for you. Never commit to a practice that isn't healthy, and never hold anything inside of yourself that needs to get out.

Clothing, accessories, tools and weapons can be expressions of who you are, but they are not extensions of who you are.

Do not be attached to possessions. Possessions are to be used, enjoyed, and discarded. Attachment is for people.

Keep in mind the difference between ignorance and stupidity. Everyone is allowed to not know things: no one knows everything, and most people are specialized.

When you encounter something you do not understand, allow someone who does understand it to make decisions, but only if you would normally trust them to make decisions about things you do understand.

Learn.

Grow.

Never owe anyone anything, never let anyone owe anything to you. Give gifts freely, accept gifts freely. If you cannot buy something with the money you have in your hand, you can't afford it.

Occasionally, in cases of dire emergency, a friend may loan something to you. Pay them back as soon as you can. If they try to charge you interest, they are no longer your friend.

Establish a routine of not having a routine.
If you find yourself doing the same thing the
same way more than twice in a row, find
something - anything - else to do.

Live in such a way that if you die young, they will still say at your funeral that you lived a full life.

A barbarian's fighting style is best described as "whatever works". Hitting something in the face with a sharp object very hard over and over again usually works.

If something doesn't work, stop doing
it, and try doing something else.

Never split the party.

Never trust statues.

Don't worry about diet.
Eat different food every day, your
guts will take care of themselves.

Don't worry about exercise.
Do different activities every day, your
muscles will take care of themselves.

If you feel bad, sort out why. If it is due to a specific problem, try to solve it. If you cannot solve it, you must understand and accept that you will feel bad for a time.

If you feel bad without a specific reason, get out and do things. Try different things until you find something that makes you not feel bad any more.

Your mind is affected by your body, and your body
is an animal. Lack of good food, lack of exercise and
lack of sleep will make you grumpy and negative.
It is your responsibility to maintain yourself.

Just as there are some monsters you cannot defeat without special weapons or a team of combatants, there may be some problems with yourself that you cannot solve on your own. A truly strong warrior knows when to change tactics. Remember: whatever works.

If you have more than you need,
use it to help others. Greed is a sin.

If you have less than you need, accept
help from others. Pride is a sin.

Stay hydrated.

Never pass up an opportunity
to wash your face and hands.

Children fear monsters.
Adults fear becoming monstrous.

Never fear pain or death.
Both are inevitable.

Remember: the point of a fight is to disable or destroy your opponent, not to punish them or to show off. End your fights as quickly as possible, and ensure the final result is not in doubt.

If you don't have to hit something, don't hit it.
If you do have to hit something, hit it as hard
as you can, and don't stop until it's down.

Trust your eyes over your brain.

Trust your heart over your eyes.

In times of chaos, act first.

In times of order, act last.

Regardless of whether you actually are the biggest and strongest, behave as though you believe you are the biggest and strongest. Act how you would want the biggest and strongest person to act.

When you're the biggest and the strongest, a smaller, weaker person trying to insult you is a funny joke, and should be treated as such.

Good people can do bad things sometimes.
You can tell they're still good people if they
try to make things right after their mistake
is pointed out. Be quick to forgive.

This includes yourself.

You may have noticed that some of the advice
in this book is contradictory. Most of the advice
you will receive in your life is contradictory.
It is useful anyway.

Live.
Live as much as you can.

-About the Authours-

Vak is an orcish barbarian who has been going on adventures since her twelfth summer. She has lots of scars and tattoos. She once killed a zombie dragon that was forty feet from nose to tail and could breathe clouds of plague gas.

Bembobimbom "Beebee" Littlewhistle is a halfling bard who has worked with Vak for three years. She sings, she dances, she tells tales, and - in this case - she writes and draws. Beebee once killed an alligator with a really nasty eye infection.

Mason "Tailsteak" Williams is a Canadian cartoonist, primarily known for his webcomics One Over Zero, Leftover Soup, and Forward. He is absolutely MERCILESS when it comes to mosquitoes.

Made in the USA
Middletown, DE
30 July 2023

35957721R00038